The Scary Tree

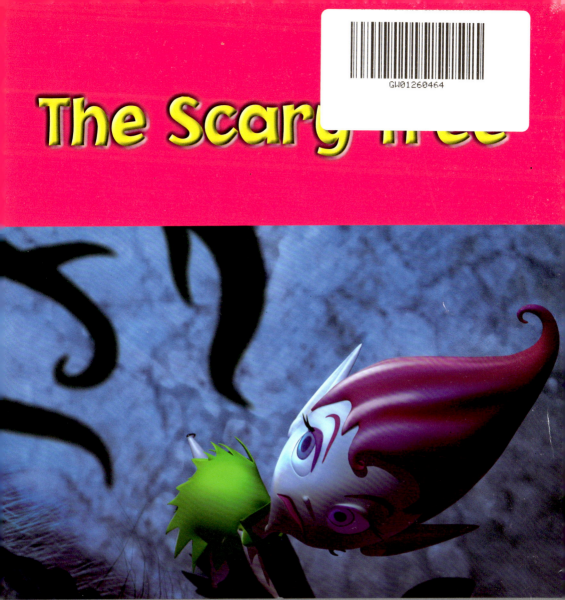

Written by Lisa Thompson

Pictures by Luke Jurevicius and Arthur Moody

In the forest, there was
a very scary tree.

The moon shone on the scary tree,
and made it look like a monster.

Binks was going home past the scary tree. She looked up.

The tree looked like a monster coming to get her.

Binks was scared.
She ran all the way home.

One day, there was a storm.
The wind shook the scary tree.

"I am not scared," said Hector.
But then a big seed fell on his head.

"Ow!" he said, and he ran home to
his bridge.

One day, it began to rain.

"My wings will get wet,"
said Dash.
"I am going to hide under the
scary tree."

But the tree shook the rain
all over her.

"Oh no!" she said.
"Now I can't fly!"

Big Eyes liked trees, but he
did not like the scary tree.

"I cannot make my nest
in this tree," he said.
"It is too scary for me
to sleep here."

In spring, the sun came out and there were leaves all over the scary tree.

It did not look scary now.

"I am going to pick some leaves for my dinner," said Gog.

"Come and sit under the scary tree with me," said Gog.

"It is not scary now," said Binks. "It is the best place to sit on a sunny day."

14

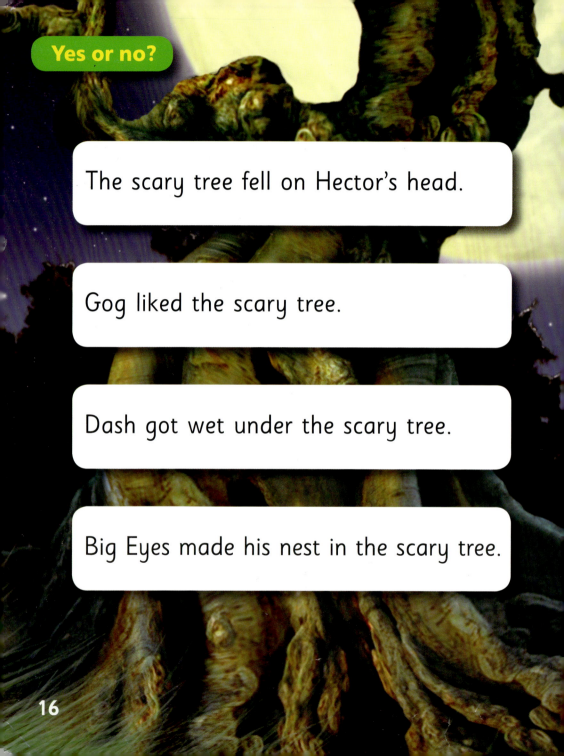

The scary tree fell on Hector's head.

Gog liked the scary tree.

Dash got wet under the scary tree.

Big Eyes made his nest in the scary tree.